Jacqueline Wilson's

adapted for the stage by Emma Reeves

OBERON BOOKS
LONDON

WWW.OBERONBOOKS.COM

This adaptation first published in 2014 by Oberon Books Ltd
521 Caledonian Road, London N7 9RH
Tel: +44 (0) 20 7607 3637 / Fax: +44 (0) 20 7607 3629
e-mail: info@oberonbooks.com
www.oberonbooks.com

Hetty Feather copyright © Jacqueline Wilson, 2009

Stage adaptation © Emma Reeves, 2014

Reprinted in 2015

A catalogue record for this book is available from the British
Library.

PB ISBN: 978-1-78319-176-5
E ISBN: 978-1-78319-675-3

Characters

Hetty Feather was originally performed by six actors and two musicians, but it could also be performed by a larger cast. The lines credited to the 'Ensemble' are divided between the actors and can spoken by any individual member of the company, or the full company together. The musicians are onstage throughout.

In order of appearance:

HETTY

ENSEMBLE

MOTHERS:
MOTHER1 MOTHER2
MOTHER3 MOTHER4

MATRON BOTTOMLY

NURSES:
NURSE1 NURSE2
NURSE3 NURSE4 NURSE5

NURSE WINNIE

GIDEON

CAB DRIVER

CARRIER

GUARD

SAM

PEG

JEM

SAUL

MUSICIANS

ELIZA

CHINO

CIRCUS PERFORMERS:
CIRCUS PERFORMER1   CIRCUS PERFORMER2
CIRCUS PERFORMER3

ELEPHANT HANDLER

RINGMASTER

HERCULES

MADAME ADELINE

FOUNDLING GIRLS:
HARRIET   MONICA
SHEILA   SARAH

IDA

RICH LADY1
RICH LADY2

RICH MAN1
RICH MAN2

BOYS:
BOY1   BOY2
BOY3   BOY4

MALE TEACHER

LITTLE GIRLS:
LITTLE GIRL1   LITTLE GIRL2

BARKER1

BARKER2

SISSY

GENTLEMAN

PASSERS-BY

URCHIN1   URCHIN2

BOBBY

Hetty Feather was first performed at the Rose Theatre, Kingston upon Thames on 5 April 2014.

The adaptation was devised by Emma Reeves, Sally Cookson and the Hetty Feather company.

The cast was as follows:

Hetty Feather	Phoebe Thomas
Jem/Matron Bottomly	Matt Costain
Peg/Ida	Sarah Goddard
Madame Adeline	Nikki Warwick
Saul	Isaac Stanmore
Gideon	Paul Mundell
Musicians	Seamus H Carey
	Luke Potter
Understudy	Jenanne Redman

Creative

Director	Sally Cookson
Adaptor	Emma Reeves
Composer	Benji Bower
Designer	Katie Sykes
Costume Supervisor	Jennie Falconer
Lighting	Aideen Malone
Sound	Leigh Davies
Aerial Director	Gwen Hales
Additional Composition	Seamas H Carey & Luke Potter

Produced by The Rose Theatre Kingston, William Archer for Bob & Co, Kenny Wax and Novel Theatre

ACT ONE

SCENE 1 – HETTY OPENING

A simple, circus-themed set which can be used to create multiple locations. Rigging for aerial work – a hanging hoop, ropes, silks. There are no set changes – performers move items to create locations as necessary. The action flows smoothly, moving effortlessly between the prosaic reality of HETTY's life and the limitless soaring of her imagination.

The ENSEMBLE enter. They lift HETTY into the aerial hoop. Music begins:

HETTY

Everyone says you can't remember back to when you were a baby.
They're wrong. What they mean is, they can't remember. But I can. I can remember everything…
I remember the moment I was born. Fighting my way out…
I remember when my mother held me in her arms for the first time. I looked up into her big blue eyes – just like mine – and I knew then, that she loved me more than anything in the world.
She did. That's what matters. Everything that happened afterwards…well, none of it was her fault.
She loved me so much it hurt. She would hold me close and stroke my hair – even though it's red.

(Sings.)
I will love you all the day
In my heart you'll always stay
Even if I have to stray
Over the hills and far away…

Say my name. The special name that you gave me. It must have been beautiful, like you – and I'm sure it was blue, like our eyes. Maybe it was…

ENSEMBLE
Bluebell.

HETTY
Bluebell. Or –

7

ENSEMBLE
Sky.

HETTY
Sky. Maybe I'm –

ENSEMBLE
Forget-me-not.

HETTY
Forget-me-not... Or –

ENSEMBLE
Ocean.

HETTY
Ocean... Maybe I'm ...?

ENSEMBLE
Azure.

HETTY
Azure... Or...

ENSEMBLE
Indigo.
Aquamarine.
Lapis Lazuli.
Violet.

HETTY
Or...

ENSEMBLE *(IDA)*.
Sapphire.

HETTY
Sapphire... I know I said I could remember everything,
but that's the one thing I can't remember. My real name.
But it doesn't really matter. Because when you don't know
who you are, you can be anyone you want to be. And,
whoever I am, this is my story.

SCENE 2 – HETTY'S MOTHER LOOKS FOR WORK

HETTY *(CONT'D.)*
Picture me as my mother.

*HETTY gets down from the hoop. She is dressed in a hat and coat and
handed BABY HETTY.*

Mother did everything she could to keep us together.
(As her mother.)
Please. Have you got any work? I'll do anything.

ENSEMBLE
Can you scrub? Can you polish? Can you lift? Can you
bend? Can you chop? Can you dig? Can you make? Can
you mend? Can you fetch? Can you carry? Can you clean?
Can you tend? Can you work?

BABY HETTY cries. The ENSEMBLE react, appalled:

ENSEMBLE
There is no work for you.

HETTY
Mother was desperate...

ENSEMBLE
Roll up, roll up, you desperate mothers.
Win a new life for your child!
Are you and your baby starving to death?
Has your employer dismissed you without a character?
Then hurry, hurry to the Foundling Hospital.
You never know – you may be one of the lucky ones.
Take your places for the Foundling Hospital Lottery.
With your genial hostess, Matron Bottomly.

MATRON BOTTOMLY appears.

SCENE 3 – FOUNDLING HOSPITAL LOTTERY

MATRON BOTTOMLY
Applicants, present your infants. Form an orderly queue.
I will not tolerate pushing, jostling or disorder of any kind
– I said, no pushing. Never mind if you are first or last – all
are equal in the Foundling Hospital Lottery. Begin.

MOTHER1
Please! Will you take my son? My little William?

MATRON BOTTOMLY
Take a ball.

MOTHER1 takes a black ball.

MOTHER1
Black...what does that mean?

MATRON BOTTOMLY
What do you think it means, you silly girl? We can't accept every baby.

MOTHER1
No. I can't look after him!

MATRON BOTTOMLY
Your lot has been drawn. The decision is final. You may not appeal, nor dispute, nor ask for a second chance –

MOTHER1
– But you don't understand –

MATRON BOTTOMLY
– And don't even think about abandoning the child.

MOTHER1
I wouldn't –

MATRON BOTTOMLY
Police officers are patrolling this neighbourhood and you will be caught. Next.

MOTHER2 takes a red ball.

MOTHER2
Red...what does that mean?

MATRON BOTTOMLY
That's a maybe. Don't go away – if a baby fails my inspection you may be in luck. Next.

MOTHER3 takes a black ball.

MOTHER3
Black...

MATRON BOTTOMLY
Next.

MOTHER3
Please. She's such a good girl, so quiet, she'll give you no trouble –

MATRON BOTTOMLY
Next.

MOTHER4 takes a black ball.

MOTHER4
Black.

MATRON BOTTOMLY
Next.

MOTHER4
She's from a good family. We're respectable people, just
down on our luck –

MATRON BOTTOMLY
Next.

MOTHER4
I'm a married woman! Not like these other trollops –

MATRON BOTTOMLY
That is enough! Next.

HETTY
And then it was our turn...

HETTY takes a white ball.
White...what does that mean?

MATRON BOTTOMLY
We'll take the child. Subject to inspection.

HETTY submits the baby for inspection by the nurses.

NURSE1
She's clean...

HETTY
Of course she's clean!

NURSE1 passes BABY HETTY to NURSE2.

NURSE2
No disease or infestation.

NURSE2 passes the baby to NURSE WINNIE.

NURSE WINNIE
She's no bigger than a twist of sugar.

HETTY
No, but she's strong!

MOTHER2
She's scrawny –

HETTY
She's tough. She's a fighter. *(Cries, as BABY HETTY.)* Wah!

NURSE WINNIE
Well, she certainly can…
(BABY HETTY screams.)
… scream.

MATRON BOTTOMLY
Clean. No disease. Strong lungs. This child has passed the inspection.

MOTHER2
No! Please take my baby, he's strong, he's healthy.

MOTHER2 is escorted out by NURSES.

MATRON BOTTOMLY
Received, on the fifteenth of January, in the year of our lord 1876, a girl child. Number…?

NURSE WINNIE
25629.

NURSE1
25629.

NURSE2
25629.

MATRON BOTTOMLY
25629. You may leave her with us now.

HETTY
Now?

MATRON BOTTOMLY
Now or never.

HETTY *(To the baby.)*
I promise I'll be back, as soon as –

MATRON BOTTOMLY
Your child belongs to us now. You have no right to claim her, or even to see her again.

HETTY
But I thought – when I get back on my feet –

MATRON BOTTOMLY
This Hospital was not founded to play nursemaid to fallen women. If you don't want the place, there are many who do.

MATRON BOTTOMLY holds out a receipt.

HETTY
Take her.

MATRON BOTTOMLY drops the receipt. WINNIE, MATRON and the NURSES leave with the baby.

HETTY
Please forgive me. I love you, I love you so much…

HETTY picks up the receipt and tucks it into her costume.

HETTY
And so my mother left. And I was alone, in this great big grey stone building…
(Crying, as BABY HETTY.)
Wah!

SCENE 4 – HETTY IS NAMED

NURSE WINNIE enters, holding BABY HETTY. She's trying to feed her.

NURSE WINNIE
Settle down, settle down… Please, little one, try to feed…

HETTY
You're not my mother. I WANT MY MOTHER!

MATRON BOTTOMLY enters.

MATRON BOTTOMLY
What's all this ungodly noise?

NURSE WINNIE
It's 25629, Matron.

MATRON BOTTOMLY
What a temper! Ah, she has red hair, I see. Hardly surprising. Is she still not feeding?

NURSE WINNIE
No, Matron.

MATRON BOTTOMLY
Don't waste your time on a hopeless case. You have other children to attend to. This one's not long for this world. She had better be christened at once. She'll need a name.

MATRON BOTTOMLY and NURSE WINNIE talk to each other, ignoring HETTY:

HETTY
I've got a name. A beautiful name.

NURSE WINNIE
… The last child was a G. Gideon.

HETTY
Blue, like my eyes.

MATRON BOTTOMLY
We need a name beginning with H.

HETTY
Sky – Azure –

NURSE WINNIE
Helen? Helen is a beautiful name –

HETTY
– Bluebell –

MATRON BOTTOMLY
She's no Helen.

NURSE WINNIE
Holly?

MATRON BOTTOMLY
Too heathen.

HETTY
– Forget-Me-Not –

NURSE WINNIE
Henrietta?

HETTY
– Sapphire – Emerald – Diamond –

MATRON BOTTOMLY
Henrietta's too fancy. She needs a good, plain, honest name. Hattie…

HETTY *(Unimpressed.)*
Hattie?

MATRON BOTTOMLY
… Hester…

HETTY
Hester?!

MATRON BOTTOMLY
... Hetty. Yes. Hetty.

HETTY
Hetty?! THAT'S NOT MY NAME!

NURSE WINNIE
Goodness, I never heard such a big noise from such a tiny
girl – why, you're light as a feather.

MATRON BOTTOMLY
Feather. There we are. Hetty Feather.

MATRON BOTTOMLY goes.

NURSE WINNIE *(Fond.)*
Hetty Feather.

NURSE WINNIE goes. HETTY is alone.

HETTY
Hetty. Feather.

The ENSEMBLE chase HETTY with feathers.

HETTY
Stop it! Leave me alone! Go away!

HETTY blows the feathers away.

HETTY
I was only a few days old and I'd lost everything.
My home, my mother – even my name.

SCENE 5 – JOURNEY TO HAVENFORD

GIDEON is clinging to a ladder.

GIDEON
Help. Help me?

HETTY
Who are you?

GIDEON
Who are you?

NURSE WINNIE places BABY GIDEON and BABY HETTY in a basket.

NURSE WINNIE
Hetty, this is Master Gideon Smeed. He's going to be your new foster brother. Move over Hetty, make room.

HETTY
Gideon Smeed. Is that your real name?

GIDEON
I don't know. What is this place? What's your name?

HETTY
This is the Foundling Hospital.
(Reluctantly.)
And I think I'm Hetty Feather.

GIDEON
Hetty Feather??

WINNIE picks up the basket and carries it through the Hospital.

What's happening? Where are we going?

HETTY
I don't know.

GIDEON
I don't like this, Hetty Feather. Make it stop.

HETTY
I wish I could.

NURSE WINNIE
Driver!

A hansom CAB DRIVER slides down a rope:

CAB DRIVER
Foundling Hospital? Going to Waterloo?

NURSE WINNIE gives the basket to the CAB DRIVER.

NURSE WINNIE *(To the CAB DRIVER.)*
They're on the 12.30 to Havenford. They'll be met at the station.
(To the babies.)
Bye bye, Hetty and Gideon. Be good for your new foster mother.

GIDEON
What did she say?

HETTY
I think we're getting a new mother...

GIDEON
I don't understand.

HETTY
Nor do I. I don't need a mother, I've already got one!

The CAB DRIVER hands the baby-basket to a CARRIER. The basket is passed around.

CAB DRIVER
12.30 to Havenford? They'll be met at the station.

CARRIER
Right you are.

The baby baskets are carried onto the train.

GIDEON
I'm scared.

HETTY
I know.

GIDEON
I'm wet.

HETTY
I know!

GIDEON
How much further, Hetty Feather?

HETTY
I don't know...

HETTY / GIDEON
What's happening....?

CARRIER
All aboard!

The train starts to travel.

ENSEMBLE
London Bridge, Lewisham, Blackheath, Charlton. Abbey Wood, Dartford, Greenhithe.

GUARD
The train will divide, please be in the front four coaches for –

ENSEMBLE
Gravesend, Higham, Cuxton, Strood. Rochester,
Chatham, Gillingham, Rainham. Newington,
Sittingbourne, Faversham. Last stop – Havenford.

*The train arrives. The CARRIER hands the baby-basket to SAM,
the CART DRIVER.*

SAM
Waterloo train? For Peg?

CARRIER
Yes. Two little skinny ones. Be surprised if they last the
winter. 'Specially the girl.

SAM
Peg'll sort 'em out.

GIDEON
What's he saying?

HETTY
I don't know. I don't like it.

HETTY and GIDEON are driven in SAM's (very slow) cart.

GIDEON
What's that smell?

HETTY
I don't know.

GIDEON
What's that sound?

HETTY
I don't know.

GIDEON
I'm still wet.

HETTY
Me too.

SCENE 6 – MEETING PEG

The cart stops.

SAM
Whoah there. All right there, Peg.

PEG

Afternoon, Sam.

SAM

Two from the Foundling. Looks like you're going to have a houseful again.

SAM takes the basket and meets PEG.

PEG

Lovely. It's been too quiet round here since Bess and Nora went.

SAM

Well it won't be quiet no more. This one here – she's only a bit of a thing but she's a shocker for the screaming.

PEG

Oh well, it shows she's got spirit. Let's have a squint at her, then.

SAM

There's a little gentleman friend in there as well.

PEG looks at the name tag attached to HETTY.

PEG

Hetty – Feather... Hello my little red-head... And Gideon Smeed... Well, hello young man.
(To SAM.)
It's a bit of a challenge, two little ones together, but I dare say I'll manage.

SAM

If anyone can do it, you can. You're a wonder with the scrawny ones.

PEG

I'll need to be. Look at these two! Not enough meat on them to bake into a pie!

GIDEON / HETTY *(Wail.)*

She's going to eat us!

PEG

Now, let's take you home for tea.

GIDEON / HETTY

Aaaargh!

Music. PEG takes the babies home:

PEG

Jem! Saul! Come and meet your new brother and sister!

JEM swings in on a rope.

Jem! Take little Hetty for me. Ain't she tiny? You were twice her size as a baby.

PEG hands BABY HETTY to JEM.

JEM

Hello, little Hetty. I'm your big brother Jem.

HETTY

Jem…

PEG

Look at that smile! I think she likes you.

HETTY

I think so, too…

SAUL looks over.

PEG

Saul, come and meet the new babies.

SAUL

Babies? But I'm your baby.

PEG

You're all my babies.

JEM

I'm not, I'm four.

PEG

This is Gideon, and this is little Hetty –

SAUL

I don't care. I don't want them. Take them back.

PEG

He don't mean it, my lambkins.

SAUL

I do mean it! She's my mother.
Mine!

JEM

Don't mind Saul. He's just grumpy.

JEM gives the HETTY BABY to PEG. She exits with both babies.

HETTY

I didn't mind Saul. I didn't mind anything. I had a home and a mother. And Jem. As the years went by, and I grew up, I felt as if I'd lived there forever.

SCENE 7 – HETTY AND JEM MONTAGE

Music (Over the Hills and Far Away.)

MUSICIANS

I will love you all the day,
In my heart you'll always stay
Even if I have to stray
Over the hills and far away.

HETTY climbs onto JEM's back. They play. HETTY 'shoots' JEM. He plays dead:

HETTY

Jem? Jem!

JEM leaps up, making HETTY jump. They continue to play.

PEG enters with mugs of milk. SAUL limps in behind her.

PEG

Hetty! Gideon! Saul! Milk!

HETTY and GIDEON run to PEG. She hands them mugs of milk.

PEG

There, my lambkins. Drink up and get big and strong.

HETTY

I am big and strong!

PEG

You're tiny. You're my little baby bird.

PEG goes in with the mugs.

SCENE 8 – BABY BIRDS

SAUL *(Scornful.)*

'My little baby bird.'

HETTY

I want to be a baby bird! Baby birds can fly…

HETTY takes a rope and swings around. She grabs GIDEON.

HETTY
> Come on Gideon! Let's be baby birds together.

GIDEON
> Why?

HETTY
> Because! You have to picture. Imagine – we're baby birds, safe in our nest, high up in the treetops. Are you picturing it?

GIDEON
> Yes...

HETTY
> But Mother Bird has to teach us to fly. So she takes us to the very edge of the nest – and then she pushes us out!

GIDEON and HETTY swing on the ropes. Flying music.

GIDEON
> Pushes us out?

HETTY
> Yes! And we're falling, falling –

GIDEON
> Falling!

HETTY
> But then – we flap our wings and we fly...

ENSEMBLE *(Sings.)*
> Fly...

HETTY
> We fly so high that even the clouds are far, far below us.

GIDEON
> I don't like it. I don't want to fall.

HETTY
> You can't fall, we're flying!

GIDEON
> But I don't know how...
> *(Panics.)*
> I'm falling!

GIDEON falls to the ground. SAUL laughs at him.

SAUL
> Chicken! It wasn't even high!

GIDEON
> Hetty makes it high. When she tells me things, they seem real.

SAUL
> That's because you're a little chicken.

HETTY
> He's not!

SAUL
> You are! Chicken! Say it! 'I'm a chicken.'

HETTY
> Stop it! Don't call him that!

> *HETTY grabs SAUL's crutch. They struggle:*

HETTY
> I hate you.

SAUL
> I hate you!

HETTY
> You're a chicken!

> *HETTY wins and stands over SAUL, threatening him with the crutch.*

SAUL
> I'll tell Mother! She'll paddle you!

HETTY
> I don't care!

> *JEM enters.*

JEM
> Hetty! Saul! Gideon!

> *HETTY and SAUL struggle up. GIDEON's still crying on the floor.*

SAUL
> She started it!

HETTY
> I didn't do anything!

JEM *(To GIDEON.)*
> What's the matter with you?

JACQUELINE WILSON / EMMA REEVES

GIDEON
    I fell.

JEM
    From where?

SAUL *(Laughing.)*
    Nowhere.

GIDEON
    We were flying through the air –

JEM
    Flying through the air?

SAUL
    It was just one of Hetty's baby pretend games.

HETTY
    We were baby birds, flying the nest. I didn't mean to hurt
    anyone.

JEM
    Hetty, sometimes your picturing can be a bit too real.

HETTY
    I can't help it.

JEM
    You know what Gideon's like. He gets frightened.

GIDEON
    I get frightened.

HETTY
    Will you picture with me?

JEM
    I'm not being a baby bird.

HETTY
    You don't have to. You can be a squirrel.

JEM
    A squirrel?

HETTY
    Yes! They climb trees and jump from branch to branch –
    just like you.

    JEM climbs up. HETTY follows.

HETTY

Jem! Wait for me!

They climb into the squirrel house.

SCENE 9 – SQUIRREL HOUSE

HETTY *(CONT'D.)*

We're squirrels. And this is our squirrel house. Hello Mr. Squirrel.

JEM

Hello.

HETTY

This is our dinner. Mmm, acorns. Go on, eat up…

JEM reluctantly pretends to take a bite.

HETTY

Mmm… Delicious. And now it's time to feed our babies.

JEM

Babies?!

HETTY

Yes. They're hungry. And cold. You need to cuddle them.

JEM

I'm not cuddling that, it's just leaves and mud.

HETTY

Just pretend. Please…

JEM climbs. HETTY follows.

JEM is carving in the tree trunk.

HETTY

One baby, two babies, three babies……What are you doing?

JEM

Carving my name. See. J – E – M. Jem.

HETTY

Jem!

JEM

Do you want me to carve your name?

HETTY

Yes!

JEM
    H is for Hetty.

HETTY
    H.

JEM
    E.

HETTY
    E.

JEM
    T.

HETTY
    T.

GIDEON
    Can I play?

JEM
    Gideon!

HETTY
    No! This is our squirrel house. Mine and Jem's.

GIDEON
    Can't I see it too?

HETTY
    All right, just you.

    GIDEON climbs. JEM and HETTY help him:

JEM
    Go on Gideon, get your foot on the branch.

HETTY
    No, the higher one! Reach up!

JEM
    Come on, Gideon!

HETTY
    Go on, Gid!

    SAUL arrives.

SAUL
    I made it. I'm here. Can I play too?

HETTY
Not you. Go away.

SAUL
No, I'm playing. How do you get up?
(Climbing.) I can do it...

HETTY
Get down!

SAUL
I did it! – Urgh, what's this mess? Leaves and dirt.

HETTY
That's not dirt, they're my babies.

SAUL
It looks like pig poo!

JEM
It's just mud.

SAUL
Pig poo! Pig poo babies!

HETTY
Stop it.

SAUL
Urgh! Dirty Hetty, playing with pig poo!

HETTY
Don't talk like that about my BABIES!

SAUL
You mean your pig poo!

HETTY
Stop it! Stop it! STOP IT!

HETTY pushes SAUL. He falls. And lies still.

JEM
Saul?

No response.

GIDEON
He's dead.

The others gather round SAUL.

JEM
Saul!

SAUL
I fell on my bad leg. I fell on my bad leg!

JEM
Stop it. You didn't fall far.

SAUL *(Wails.)*
Aaargh!

HETTY
Don't be a baby!

JEM tries to help SAUL up.

JEM
Gideon. Help me.

JEM picks SAUL up, motioning GIDEON to take the other side and help him walk. They limp along. SAUL turns to HETTY, malevolently.

SAUL *(To HETTY.)*
Mother's going to paddle you for this! You're going to get such a beating.

JEM
No she won't. 'Cos you won't tell her.

SAUL
I will.

JEM
Gideon, put him down.

The two boys lower SAUL to the ground.

SAUL
You can't leave me here!

JEM
Will you tell Mother it was an accident?

SAUL
No!

JEM
Come on Gideon.

SAUL
All right! All right! I'll lie. I'll say it was an accident.

JEM
Good.

JEM and GIDEON pick SAUL up and they limp back to PEG.

SAUL
Hetty, get my crutch.

HETTY picks up the crutch and trails it home.

SCENE 10 – HETTY GETS PADDLED

SAUL (CONT'D.)
(*Pathetic.*)
Mother!

PEG
Saul, love! What happened?

SAUL
Hetty pushed me out of a tree and I fell on my bad leg.

PEG
Hetty, is this true?

HETTY
Yes, but –

JEM
She didn't mean to.

GIDEON
She didn't mean to.

HETTY
I did! He called my babies pig poo!

SAUL
They were pig poo!

JEM
It wasn't high. It was just the old oak in the woods –

PEG
Just tell me, Hetty. Did you push Saul out of a tree?

HETTY
Yes I did. I'm glad. And I'd do it again.

PEG
Then you're a bad, bad girl, Hetty Feather. You're not to play in that oak tree ever again. Boys, get the bench. I'm getting my ladle.

PEG marches off. SAUL instantly stops crying and grins at HETTY.

JEM *(To SAUL.)*
You promised you wouldn't tell.

SAUL
Hetty's not the only one who lies.

HETTY
You sneaking little toad!

SAUL
Go on! Hit me! Get another paddling!

HETTY charges at SAUL and grapples with him as PEG enters.

PEG
Hetty Feather, leave Saul alone and come here!

PEG paddles HETTY.

ENSEMBLE
One two three, paddle on the bum
Ooh ah, makes you feel numb
Four five six, paddle on the bot
Ouch ee, when's it gonna stop?
Seven eight nine, paddle on the rump,
Just one more, one last big thump.
Owwww!

PEG has finished paddling HETTY:

PEG
There. I hope you've learned your lesson. Why can't you be kinder to Saul?

HETTY
Because I hate him.

PEG
You don't mean that.

HETTY
I do. I hate him more than anything in the world. I wish he'd disappear forever.

PEG
You don't know what you're saying.

HETTY
I do, I'm picturing it now. The ground will open and the Devil will crawl out and drag him to H – E – L – L...

PEG

Wash your mouth out! Don't you know that if you speak of the Devil, he will appear?

HETTY

I wish he would. The Devil would be a better brother than Saul.

PEG

Hetty Feather! In all my years, I've never known such a bad girl.

HETTY

Well, in all my years, I've never known such a bad mother!

PEG appears to be sobbing...

HETTY

Mother?

HETTY realises that PEG is laughing. She laughs and laughs:

PEG

You little imp! Come here.

HETTY goes to PEG. It hurts to sit down:

HETTY

Ow!

PEG

What am I going to do with you?

HETTY

Paddle me again, probably.

PEG

I don't like to hurt you. But you must learn to keep your passions under control.

HETTY

Why do you love Saul more than me?

PEG

I love you all the same, you silly girl.

HETTY

Will you love me forever?

PEG

Forever and more. I'll never forget you, Hetty Feather. Go on, off you go to bed.

MUSICIANS
> *I will love you all the day,*
> *In my heart you'll always stay,*
> *Even if I have to stray,*
> *Over the hills and far away.*

HETTY goes to bed, where the other children are already sleeping.

PEG laughs to herself as she remembers HETTY's words. She folds the children's clothes.

PEG
Goodnight, my lambs. Sleep well.

SCENE 11 – SAUL GOES BACK TO THE FOUNDLING HOSPITAL

Early morning. SAUL, HETTY, GIDEON and JEM are asleep.

PEG puts her coat on. She packs a bag, composes herself and goes to wake SAUL:

PEG *(CONT'D.)*
Saul? Saul, wake up, my lamb. Ssh. Come downstairs with me.

A sleepy SAUL gets up and goes to the bench with PEG.

PEG
Here's your milk, my love.

SAUL
Where are the others?

PEG
Still asleep. Don't wake them.

SAUL
Why – ?

PEG
Drink up now. We don't want to miss the train.

SAUL
Train…?

PEG
Yes. We're going on a journey, my lamb.

SAUL
Where?

PEG
We're going to London –

SAUL

London!

PEG

Ssh. Yes. To a lovely place called the Foundling
Hospital.

SAUL

Hospital? Because of my poorly leg?

PEG

It's not that kind of hospital. It's a big happy home for lots
of children who don't have mothers –

SAUL

But I've got a mother. I've got you.

HETTY has crept down and is listening to the conversation:

PEG

Oh, my love. I wish I could be your mother forever. But
you see, you belong to the Foundling Hospital. Now, let's
get your coat on…

SAUL

I don't want to go. Let me stay here with you. Please.

PEG

I can't. I'm not allowed. I have to take you back there
before you turn six. It's their rules.

SAUL

When do the rules let me come home?
(No reply.)
Mother?

HETTY

Mother? Why are you up so early?

PEG

Hetty, go back to bed –

SAUL

Hetty, she's taking me away.

HETTY

Where are you taking him?

PEG

Hush now, Hetty. I'll speak to you later.

SAUL *(To HETTY.)*
> I don't want to go! Help me.

HETTY *(To PEG.)*
> Please. You can't. I didn't mean what I said. I didn't mean it! I'm sorry!

PEG
> Hetty, don't take on so.

> *GIDEON is awake now.*

GIDEON
> What's happening? Where's Saul going?

PEG
> It's all right, Gid. Nothing to worry about.

SAUL
> I don't want to go.

PEG *(To SAUL.)*
> Don't fret, my lambkin. You're going to a good place.

HETTY
> What place?

PEG *(Calls.)*
> Jem! Look after the little ones.
> We have to catch our train. Come along, Saul.

> *PEG ushers SAUL out.*

SAUL *(As he goes, sotto.)*
> Hetty…

> *SAUL and PEG depart.*

SCENE 12 – WAITING FOR PEG

Music. HETTY, GIDEON and JEM in the house together, waiting for PEG. They play paper-scissors-stone.

GIDEON
> I'm hungry. When's Mother coming back?

JEM
> She said she'd be back by teatime.

HETTY
> It is teatime.

They all look out.

JEM *(Looks.)*
Someone's coming!

The children run to look for PEG:

GIDEON
Can you see her?

HETTY
Is it Mother?

JEM
It's a woman.

HETTY
Is Saul with her?

JEM
Wait 'till she comes past the tree.

GIDEON
That's her coat.

JEM
It's Mother!

HETTY / JEM / GIDEON
Mother! Mother!

The children run to meet PEG. They hug her.

PEG
Come on, let me get inside then.

HETTY *(Desperately hoping.)*
Where's Saul? Is Saul coming back?

PEG
No, my lamb. He lives at the Foundling Hospital now.

GIDEON
Did he cry when you left him?

PEG
Yes. He cried.

HETTY
A lot?

PEG
Yes.

HETTY

Did you cry? You did, didn't you?

PEG

I did. But there's no cause to grieve over Saul.
The Foundling Hospital is a wonderful place –

In her basket, ELIZA begins to cry.

PEG *(To the BABY ELIZA.)*

Hush, my lambkin…

GIDEON

What's that?

HETTY

Who's that?

PEG picks up the baby.

PEG

This is your new sister. Little Eliza. Eliza, this is Gideon.

GIDEON

Hello Eliza.

PEG

And this is Hetty, and this –

JEM

Hello Eliza. I'm your big brother Jem.

ELIZA stops crying and smiles at JEM.

ELIZA

Hello, Jem.

PEG

I think she likes you…

JEM takes ELIZA and walks around soothing her.

HETTY

You left Saul in that place. And brought her back instead?

PEG

It's not my choice, Hetty. If I had my way I'd keep all of you.

Her words sink in:

HETTY

So – you can't keep all of us?

The children look at PEG, *anxious for her response:*

PEG *(Finally.)*

No.

GIDEON

Do we have to go to that hospital too?

PEG

Not yet. Not until you're nearly six.

HETTY

But Jem's nine!

PEG

Jem didn't come from the Foundling.

HETTY

Where did he come from then?

PEG

Jem's my own child. My own flesh and blood.

HETTY

I thought we were all your own children.

PEG

To me you are. But you Foundling children are very blessed. When you grow up together in that Hospital, they'll teach you all sorts of clever things. Reading, writing, fine sewing. They'll train you up to be a servant girl.

HETTY

I don't want to be a servant girl!

GIDEON

Will I be a servant girl?

PEG

No, Giddy. You'll be a brave soldier.

GIDEON

I'd like to be a servant girl.

HETTY

I'd like to be a brave soldier! I want to go adventuring.

PEG

You're a strange pair. Now, you two, run off and play. I've got to see to Eliza.

HETTY climbs up into the squirrel house and cocoons herself in the silks:

GIDEON
> At least we'll be together.
> *(But she's gone.)*
> Hetty? Hetty?

JEM also starts looking for HETTY:

GIDEON / JEM
> Hetty!

SCENE 13 – JEM MAKES A PROMISE

JEM
> Hetty Feather! Hetty! I know you're up there.

No reply. JEM climbs up.

JEM
> Hetty. I'm not going away so you may as well talk to me.

HETTY
> Why didn't you tell me?

JEM
> I didn't know.

HETTY
> They're going to take me away.

JEM
> Not yet.

HETTY
> But they will one day.

JEM
> As soon as I'm old enough, I'll come and get you. We'll run away together and nobody will ever catch us. And we'll live here in the squirrel house.

HETTY
> And be Mr and Mrs Squirrel and live on acorns and look after our squirrel babies together. Promise me? Promise we will?

JEM
> I promise.

They touch hands. A rumbling sound.

SCENE 14 – THE CIRCUS ARRIVES

HETTY
What's that?

JEM
What?

HETTY
That noise.

JEM *(Listens.)*
Sounds like an earthquake.

HETTY
Is the ground going to eat us?

JEM
No.

HETTY
Is the world ending?

JEM
No!

HETTY
But if it does, will you save me?

JEM
Of course I will. Just stay there. Hold onto your branch.

HETTY
The trees are moving. Look.

JEM
That's not a tree.

HETTY
What is it?

JEM
I don't know…

HETTY
It's bigger than a tree. It's bigger than the hills. It's –
a MONSTER!

JEM
There's no such thing as monsters.

39

HETTY
 Yes there is. LOOK!

ELIJAH the elephant, CHINO the clown and the other CIRCUS PERFORMERS arrive.

CIRCUS PERFORMERS
 Prepare to be excited delighted and maybe even frighted *(Ooh ah.)*
 Magical tragical fantastical
 Truly you will see the newly unimaginable.
 Wow. That's amazing.

CIRCUS PERFORMER1
 Roll up. Roll up.

CIRCUS PERFORMER2
 Tanglefield's Travelling Circus is here!

CIRCUS PERFORMER3
 Prepare to be amazed and astounded. You will see great wonders.

HETTY
 What wonders? Where?

CHINO
 Pennyman's fields. Shows at three, five and seven. Extra show on Saturdays.

HETTY
 What's your monster called?

CIRCUS PERFORMER3
 Elijah. He's the largest elephant in the world.

HETTY
 Elephant.

JEM
 What does he eat?

CHINO
 Anything.

HETTY
 I've got a bit of cake.

CIRCUS PERFORMER3
 He loves cake.

JEM and HETTY feed the elephant as the other performers continue their spiel:

CIRCUS PERFORMER1
Hurry, hurry to Tanglefield's Travelling Circus!

CIRCUS PERFORMER2
Gasp at the skill of Wild Wally McCall, the seven-fingered knife juggler.

CIRCUS PERFORMER1
Shudder at the shocking contortions of Elastica, the incredible bendy woman.

CHINO
Chuckle at the comic capers of Chino the clown.

CIRCUS PERFORMER3
A parade of marvels will unfold before your very eyes.

CIRCUS PERFORMER1
It's spectacular.

CIRCUS PERFORMER2
It's phenomenal.

CHINO
It's threepence each, no discounts, no refunds.

JEM and HETTY are dismayed.

HETTY
But we don't have any money.

CHINO *(To the others.)*
C'mon lads.

The circus packs up and heads off.

CIRCUS PERFORMERS *(Singing as they go.)*
Prepare to be excited delighted and maybe even frighted
(Ooh ah.)
Magical tragical fantastical
Truly you will see the newly unimaginable.

JEM and HETTY chase the departing circus:

HETTY
No – wait! Don't go. I want to see the circus.

CHINO
You don't pay, you don't see nowt.

41

JACQUELINE WILSON / EMMA REEVES

The troupe go to set up the circus tent.

SCENE 15 – SNEAKING INTO THE CIRCUS

HETTY *(To JEM.)*
    I have to see the circus. I have to. Jem!

JEM
    Ssh.

The circus tent is pitched.

HETTY
    I won't shush. I need to see Tanglefield's Travelling Circus.

JEM
    That's why you need to shush. Come on. We'll sneak in
    round the back. I'll go first, then you follow. Got it?

HETTY
    Got it.

JEM and HETTY try to creep into the tent.

HETTY
    We're missing it!

JEM
    We're not missing it.

HETTY
    I can hear clapping.

JEM
    There's no point in being caught, is there? Then we won't
    see nothing. Just wait for our chance –

They hide as CHINO throws a child out with great brutality:

CHINO
    Get out! Get out! I won't have you little varmints sneaking
    in here. You pay or you get Chino's boot up your arse.

BOY
    Wouldn't watch it if you paid me, Mr Chino!

The BOY blows a raspberry at CHINO and runs off.

JEM
    Be very careful…

HETTY and JEM creep over to the other side of the tent.

42

An ELEPHANT HANDLER comes out and feeds ELIJAH:

ELEPHANT HANDLER
Come on Elijah, feeding time. There you go. Get it down you. Good boy… Right, that's enough. Showtime.

The ELEPHANT HANDLER goes into the tent.

JEM
Last chance. Just act casual.

JEM and HETTY sneak in.

SCENE 16 – THE CIRCUS SHOW

MASSIVE APPLAUSE as the TUMBLERS finish their act with a great flourish. Gasps and cheers of delight from the audience. The TUMBLERS take their bows and leave.

RINGMASTER
Legend tells of a great hero. The strongest man who ever lived. Please welcome the mighty – Hercules!

HERCULES enters and poses, displaying his muscles. Assistants bring on a dumbbell. HERCULES picks it up and lifts it above his head. Then picks it up with one hand.

HERCULES
I am Hercules, the strongest man in the world. Thank you.

Applause. HERCULES exits.

SCENE 17 – MADAME ADELINE'S ACT

RINGMASTER
Now, Tanglefield's Travelling Circus brings you the thrilling bareback riding of the Queen of the Cossacks – the peerless, the fearless Madame Adeline.

MADAME ADELINE enters and climbs into the aerial hoop.

MADAME ADELINE *(Russian accent.)*
I am Madame Adeline, the greatest rider in the world. And these are my magnificent horses.

MADAME ADELINE performs some aerial moves as the horses gallop.

MADAME ADELINE
Ladies and Gentlemen, presenting Sultan!
An Arab thoroughbred stallion. Presented to me by Sheik of Araby as token of his esteem. Hup!

Tsarina!
My proud princess. Her great-great-great grandfather
belong to Catherine the Great.
Diabolo!
El Diabolo! They called him the very Devil himself.
Nobody could tame him but me.
And the best for last – my little Pirate. Sometimes she will
perform, sometimes she will not. Who knows?

PIRATE does a poo.

MADAME ADELINE
Ladies and gentlemen, my horses!
Ha! This is the way Madame Adeline rides. Now, children,
who dares to come up here and ride with me? I need a
volunteer. A little girl or boy with spirit, with courage, with
fire in their soul –

HETTY
Me! Me! Pick me, I've got all of those things!

HETTY runs onto stage and trips up.

MADAME ADELINE
Ah, here's a little acrobat! How old are you, my child?

HETTY
Five.

MADAME ADELINE
Only five, ladies and gentlemen – and she dares to ride
with Madame Adeline.

HETTY
Yes!

MADAME ADELINE
A round of applause for this brave little one. Tsarina!
Hup!

TSARINA the horse kneels down.

MADAME ADELINE
Climb up on Tsarina and come up here. One, two, three,
and hup!

HETTY climbs up and joins MADAME ADELINE in her act:

MADAME ADELINE
Now swing your legs forward, backwards, and hup!
Beautiful!
(To HETTY.)
Well done, my precious child. Now, let go. Don't worry.
I have you, you're safe.

HETTY lets go, balances.

MADAME ADELINE
Look at this, ladies and gentlemen! What a little star.

They ride the horses.

MADAME ADELINE
Now, my little star. It is time for you to shine!

HETTY and MADAME ADELINE perform an acrobatic aerial routine.

MADAME ADELINE *(To audience.)*
Ladies and gentlemen – put your hands together for my little star!
(To HETTY.)
Take your bow!

Applause. HETTY bows and bows, loving it. As the circus comes to an end and the performers pack up and leave, HETTY's still bowing. The ELEPHANT HANDLER's sweeping the stage. HETTY picks up a paper star from the floor.

SCENE 18 – AFTER THE CIRCUS

ELEPHANT HANDLER
Show's over love. Haven't you got a home to go to?

JEM
Hetty! Hetty!

HETTY
Did you see? Did you see me ride with Madame Adeline?

JEM
Of course I did! You were brilliant!

HETTY *(Thrilled, to audience.)*
I was brilliant wasn't I? But Mother didn't think so.

PEG's scrubbing the floor. MADAME ADELINE's present in HETTY's imagination:

PEG
> Hetty Feather! You're the talk of the village!

HETTY
> I know.

PEG
> You're a bad girl. Cavorting in that heathen circus show!

HETTY
> I wasn't bad, I was brilliant. Madame Adeline called me...

HETTY / MADAME ADELINE
> My Little Star.

PEG
> 'Madame Adeline' is a very wicked woman. Flaunting herself half-naked in front of decent folk. She's no better than she should be.

HETTY *(To MADAME ADELINE.)*
> How could you be any better? You're the greatest rider in the whole world!

MADAME ADELINE
> My precious child...

HETTY
> I wish I was your child...
> I could be your child. I've got red hair, just like yours...
> Are you my real mother? Please say you are.

MADAME ADELINE
> My clever Little Star!

HETTY goes to JEM:

HETTY
> Jem!

JEM
> What is it?

HETTY
> I have to go back to the circus!

JEM
> You've been to the circus! Nothing's ever enough for you, is it?

46

HETTY

But Madame Adeline is my real mother.

JEM

You've been picturing again.

HETTY

She told me so!

JEM

I haven't got time for your games now. I've got chores to do.

HETTY sneaks off and out of the house.

HETTY

Madame Adeline! Madame Adeline! I'm coming!

HETTY runs frantically to the circus – but the field is empty.

HETTY

When I got to Pennyman's fields, the circus had gone.

HETTY picks up a paper star.

HETTY

I waited and waited, but Madame Adeline never came back. I waited all spring, all summer, and all autumn. And then, winter came…

SCENE 19 – GOODBYE TO JEM

PEG is dressing GIDEON and HETTY. She gives them bags.

PEG

Gideon. Hetty. Come on, my lambs. It's time to go… Jem. Say goodbye.

JEM

You don't have to say goodbye yet. I'll come with you.

PEG

You can't. I haven't got a ticket for you.

JEM

I'll hide from the ticket man.

PEG

No, Jem. I need you to look after Eliza. Now be a good lad and stay here.

HETTY

Jem! Don't forget me!

JEM

    Never! I told you, I'll come and get you just as soon as I'm old enough.

HETTY

    Remember our promise?

JEM

    I remember. I promise!

SCENE 20 – JOURNEY BACK TO LONDON

The whistle blows as HETTY, GIDEON and PEG board the train:

ENSEMBLE

    Faversham, Sittingbourne, Newington, Rainham. Gillingham, Chatham, Rochester, Strood. Cuxton, Higham, Gravesend, Greenhithe. Dartford, Abbey Wood, Charlton, Blackheath, Lewisham, London Bridge – last stop – Waterloo.

HETTY, GIDEON and PEG are jostled by crowds at the station. They travel through London and approach the Foundling Hospital with trepidation.

SCENE 21 – ARRIVAL AT THE FOUNDLING HOSPITAL

PEG

    Good afternoon. I'm Peg, from Havenford –

NURSE1 *(Interrupting.)*

    Foster mother?

PEG

    That's right, I've brought these two little 'uns –

NURSE1

    Foundling numbers?

PEG

    Oh...

PEG takes out two foundling lockets and puts one around HETTY's neck.

PEG

    25629....

NURSE1

    25629.

PEG

    Hetty Feather.

NURSE2
25629.

NURSE1
And?

PEG puts the other locket around GIDEON's neck.

PEG
25621.

NURSE1
25621.

PEG
Gideon Smeed.

NURSE2
25621.

PEG
They're such dear children. Hetty's a fiery young thing, but she's a good girl really. Such a loving heart. Now Gideon's a gentle soul. He needs a little extra cosseting –

MATRON BOTTOMLY
All are equal in the eyes of the Foundling Hospital.
We have no favourites here. Foster mothers, you may leave.

PEG hugs the children. She places their hands together and leaves. Pauses at the door:

PEG
Hetty. Look after your brother.

HETTY and GIDEON cling to each other.

HETTY
Don't worry. I promise I'll look after you.

MATRON BOTTOMLY
Foundlings, today you begin a new life. You are fortunate indeed. You will be fed, clothed and educated in a manner befitting your station in life.
It is time to put away childish things. We expect you to work hard, to show gratitude to your benefactors, and to know your place in the world. Your place is here.

NURSE1
Follow me. Girls to the left.

NURSE2
Boys to the right.

GIDEON
Hetty, don't leave me.

HETTY
If you please, Nurse, Gideon and me, we have to stay together.

NURSE1
You cannot go with your brother. The girls' wing is this way.

NURSE2
The boys' wing is this way.

HETTY
But you don't understand. He needs me –

NURSE1
Nonsense!

HETTY
It's not nonsense. I promised Mother. He's my brother.

MATRON BOTTOMLY
No more of that. Forget about your foster family. You are at the Foundling Hospital now, and you must obey our rules. Here, boys and girls live separately.

HETTY and GIDEON are dragged apart.

GIDEON
Hetty!

HETTY *(Simultaneously.)*
Gideon!

SCENE 22 – HETTY IS DRESSED AS A FOUNDLING

HETTY is dragged into the girls' wing.

NURSE1 *(To HETTY.)*
Clothes off.

HETTY
What?

NURSE2
Take your clothes off girl.

NURSE3
Don't argue.

NURSE4
Don't make a fuss.

NURSE3
Don't make us fetch Matron.

They pick her up and take her clothes.

HETTY
What are you doing with my clothes?

NURSE1
You won't need these any more.

NURSE2
They shall be disposed of.

NURSE3
They shall be burnt.

HETTY
But they're my best Sunday clothes.

NURSE3
You don't need them any more.

HETTY
Do foundling children have to walk around naked?

NURSE5
Time for your bath.

HETTY is placed in a tin bath.

HETTY
But I've had a bath. I'm clean!

NURSE1
Country clean.

NURSE2
You need a proper scrubbing.

NURSE3
To get rid of all the dirt.

NURSE4
All the filth.

NURSE5
All the nasty bugs and beasties.

JACQUELINE WILSON / EMMA REEVES

HETTY
 No – urgh, get off me!

NURSE1
 Keep still, you fiery little imp.

NURSE5
 This will quench that fire!

 The NURSES throw a bucket of water over HETTY.

HETTY
 Aargh!

NURSE2
 That will quell that temper.

NURSE3
 Now it's time to dry you, child!

NURSE4
 Keep still!

NURSES
 Keep still!

NURSE1
 Get out.

 The NURSES take HETTY out of the bath.

NURSE1
 Now for that hair.

HETTY
 My hair? What are you doing with my hair? Please?
 Don't touch my hair!

NURSE2
 All new admissions must have their hair cut off.

HETTY
 No. Please – you can't.

NURSE5
 I've never seen so much hair.

NURSE1
 Nasty, dirty hair.

NURSE2
 Crawling with lice, no doubt.

HETTY
It's not.

NURSE3
And it's red.

NURSE4
The Devil's colour.

NURSE5
It has to go.

The NURSES produce scissors. They cut her hair.

HETTY
No!

NURSE1
Now you will put on your new uniform.

HETTY
Where are my drawers?

NURSE2
You do not wear such garments here.

NURSE3
All foundlings wear exactly the same.

NURSE4
A brown dress.

NURSE5
A brown cap.

NURSE1
A tippet.

NURSE2
And boots.

NURSE1
There.

NURSES
Respectable at last.

The NURSES leave.

HETTY *(To audience.)*
My home. My mother. My brothers. My clothes. My hair.
I'd lost everything. Again.

ACT TWO

SCENE 23 – FOUNDLING HOSPITAL REGIME

Bells ring.

MATRON BOTTOMLY

Girls. Let us thank the Lord for the new day that He
has given us. As always, let us strive to please Him by
conducting ourselves with piety, industry and decorum.

*HETTY follows the other FOUNDLING GIRLS around the hospital
and into dinner.*

MATRON BOTTOMLY

Girls, let us say grace.

HETTY

Grace.

GIRLS

For what we are about to receive, may the Lord make us
truly thankful.

HETTY and the other FOUNDLING GIRLS eat their porridge.

HETTY follows the other girls through the corridor:

HETTY

Where do the boys live? When do we see them?

HARRIET

Never. We're not allowed to see the boys.

Sewing class. The other girls sew competently.

MATRON BOTTOMLY

Reconcile yourselves to the fatigue of constant labour.
Submit to your betters in everything. Happiness lies in
doing your duty in the station in which you are placed.

HETTY struggles to thread a needle, and finally pricks her finger:

HETTY

Ow!

MATRON BOTTOMLY

Hetty Feather. Get on with your needlework. We do not
tolerate indolence here.

The GIRLS walk around the Hospital again, and go to a singing class.

GIRLS *(Singing.)*
Aaahhhh…

One of the GIRLS has a surpisingly deep voice. HETTY begins to giggle.

MATRON BOTTOMLY
Who is that sinful girl who dares to laugh during our
sacred hymns? Satan will take you straight to H-E-L-L.

The GIRLS return to the dining hall.

HETTY
We never get to see the boys?

HARRIET
No. Ssh, we're not allowed to talk.

HETTY
You don't understand. Gideon needs me.

HARRIET
Who's Gideon?

HETTY
My foster brother.

HARRIET
I think I had a foster brother.

HETTY
What was his name?

HARRIET
I don't remember.
IDA serves them food.

SCENE 24 – HETTY MEETS IDA

MUSICIANS
One potato, two potato, three potato, four, five potato,
six potato, seven potato more…

IDA *(To HETTY.)*
So you're the new girl? I'm new around here too.

HETTY
They won't let me see my brother.

IDA
They have some strange rules in this place.
(HETTY nods.)
But I'm sure we'll both settle in soon. Here.

IDA gives her an extra potato.

IDA
> Extra tater.

HETTY
> Thanks, Miss. Nurse.

IDA
> Call me Ida. What's your name?

HETTY
> Hetty Feather. It's a silly name.

IDA
> I think it's a very distinctive name.
> *(Serving her butter.)*
> Extra butter.

HETTY
> Thank you.

MATRON BOTTOMLY
> Hetty Feather! No talking at meal times!

IDA
> Beg pardon Ma'am. It was my fault.

MATRON BOTTOMLY
> Who are you?

IDA
> Ida Battersea, Ma'am. It's my first day.

MATRON BOTTOMLY
> Kitchen staff do not talk to the foundlings. You must learn
> to hold your tongue, Ida Battersea.

IDA
> Yes ma'am.

IDA leaves – but stops to wink at HETTY before she goes.

SCENE 25 – READING LESSONS

The foundlings move on to a reading / writing lesson.

GIRLS
> A is for apple, B is for bear, C is for chair, D is for dog.
> A is for apple, B is for bear, C is for chair, D is for dog…

HETTY

E is for elephant! I've seen an elephant at the circus. He's got a big nose called a trunk and he's called Elijah. F is for farm, where I used to live. G is for Gideon, he's my brother. H is for Hetty, it's not my real name.

GIRLS

A is for apple, B is for bear, C is for chair, D is for dog.

HETTY

I is for Ida, she's the nicest person here. J is for Jem. He taught me to read and he's coming to save me. K is for kitchen, where Ida works. L is for lice, which I never had. M is for Mother…

GIRLS

Mother…

The GIRLS begin to sob. MATRON BOTTOMLY descends.

MATRON BOTTOMLY

What is all this nonsense?

The GIRLS push HETTY off the bench.

MATRON BOTTOMLY

Hetty Feather! Stop disrupting the class, and apply yourself to learning your letters.

HETTY

If you please Matron, I know all my letters. Jem taught me. Can I read a storybook instead?

MATRON BOTTOMLY

Storybook? We have no such things here. You will write out your alphabet again – in silence.

SCENE 26 – FOUNDLING GIRLS PLAYTIME

The bell rings. The GIRLS go outside for recreation. MONICA and SHEILA are playing together.

HETTY

Can I play?

SHEILA

No.

They run off, singing. HARRIET and SARAH are whispering secrets to each other. HETTY approaches them.

57

HETTY
What are you talking about?

SARAH
None of your business.

HARRIET
New girl.

HETTY goes off to play on her own. She plays scissors-paper-stone on her own.

HETTY
Oh! A draw! Yes! Hetty wins! Ha! Hetty wins again – I'm the best at this game!
(But the other girls are still ignoring her. She gives up. She goes off on her own. Lonely:)
Jem…

JEM
Hetty! I'm here. What are you snivelling about?

HETTY
It's horrible here, Jem. I hate it.

JEM
I know, but it won't be forever. I'm coming to save you, remember?

HETTY
You promise?

JEM
I promise. So there's nothing to cry about. You just have to wait and be patient…

SCENE 27 – EVERY DAY WAS THE SAME

HETTY *(To audience.)*
I had to be very, very patient.
Every day was the same. Wake up, wash, dress, breakfast, lessons, lavatory, dinner, darning, supper, lavatory, bed, sleep.

HETTY & ENSEMBLE
Wake up, wash, dress, breakfast, lessons, lavatory, dinner, darning, supper, lavatory, bed, sleep. Wake up, wash, dress, breakfast, lessons, lavatory, dinner, darning, supper, lavatory, bed, sleep.

SCENE 28 – SUNDAY VISITORS

HETTY

Every day was the same except Sundays. On Sundays, we all went to chapel, and afterwards, as we ate our dinner, rich people came to stare and gawp at us.

MATRON BOTTOMLY escorts the rich people in.

MATRON BOTTOMLY

Thanks to you, our benefactors, these poor deserted children are fed, clothed and well instructed in their Christian duties.

RICH LADY1

Look at the little angel in front. So neat and dainty… Here's a boiled sweet for you, my dear.

RICH MAN1

Take a stick of liquorice. This one has the most exquisite manners.

RICH MAN2

What a beautiful smile! Here, little Miss. A big piece of butterscotch. Don't eat it all at once.

HETTY realises what's going on and produces a BIG SMILE.

RICH LADY2

Oh, look at this one with the bright red hair!

RICH MAN2

She's simply enchanting. This is for you. A barley sugar twist. It matches your hair.

RICH MAN1

Delightful, delightful.

MATRON BOTTOMLY

Luncheon is served in the Governors' Room.

The BENEFACTORS leave.

HETTY

Barley sugar twist…

SHEILA and her friends surround HETTY. HETTY tries to escape but SHEILA grabs HETTY and takes her sweet.

HETTY

That's my sweet, Sheila!

SHEILA
It's mine now.

SHEILA takes the sweet and eats it. HETTY struggles with SHEILA.

GIRLS
Fight, fight fight!

SHEILA wins and pushes HETTY over.

SHEILA
F is for Feather, falling flat on her face.

SARAH
You're so funny Sheila.

SHEILA and the girls leave as IDA enters:

IDA
Hetty! What happened?

HETTY
Nothing. I fell over. These blooming boots are too big.

IDA
Well, you'll soon grow into them.
(To HETTY.)
Here. I made you some toffee. Pop it in your pocket.

HETTY
Thank you Ida!

IDA
How are you getting on with your lessons?

HETTY
I hate them. A is for apple, B is for boring. And P is for the teacher who looks like a pig face.

IDA
I know it's not easy. But you need to learn your letters –

HETTY
It is easy! I know all my letters! But they don't let us read. I want to read stories!

IDA
Stories eh…? I knew you was bright. I'll see what I can do.

HETTY
Thank you Ida!

The FOUNDLING GIRLS enter and move in a circle with HETTY.
IDA pulls HETTY aside:

IDA

Hetty. You said you wanted stories. Cook gave me this.

HETTY

What is it?

IDA

The Police Gazette.

IDA hands HETTY a POLICE GAZETTE.

HETTY

Thank you! What's it about?

IDA

I'm not much of a reader myself. But Cook says it's really thrilling.

HETTY *(Reading.)*
Police Gazette. Spine-chilling tales from the criminal underworld.

Time passes.

SCENE 29 – TIME PASSING (POLICE GAZETTE)

HETTY is reading. She hides her Police Gazette from MATRON BOTTOMLY:

MATRON BOTTOMLY

Hurry to your lessons, girls. The Devil makes work for idle hands.

IDA

Hetty. April. Police Gazette.

Time passes.

HETTY

Thank you Ida. They're wonderful!

Time passes.

IDA

May. Police Gazette. June. Police Gazette. July. Police Gazette. August. Police Gazette. September. October. Police Gazette. November. Police Gazette. December. Police Gazette. January. Police Gazette. February. Police

Gazette. March. Police Gazette. Police Gazette. October.
Police Gazette. November. Police Gazette. December.
Police Gazette.

*HETTY grows up. Her long plaits are taken down. The girls assemble
in the dormitory as HETTY reads her big pile of Police Gazettes.*

SCENE 30 – STORIES IN THE DORMITORY

*The girls lie in their dormitory beds. HETTY is reading in bed. Rustling
papers, exclaiming in shock as she reads.*

SHEILA
Hetty Feather, stop it.

HETTY
I'm just reading…

SHEILA
Well don't. We're trying to sleep.

HETTY continues to read. Lets out a gasp again.

GIRLS
Ssh / be quiet / stop it / etc.

SHEILA
Be quiet now or I'll come up there and slap you.

HETTY
Oh, sew your lips up with a darning needle Sheila.

FOUNDLINGS react – ooooh!

SHEILA
Temper, temper. Typical red-head. No self-control.

HETTY
Hold your tongue, Sheila Mayhew. Or I will lose my
temper. And then, maybe I'll do what Mad Flora Jackson
did…

SHEILA
I don't care about your stupid stories.

HARRIET
Who's mad Flora Jackson?

HETTY
I'm just reading about her in the Police Gazette.

GIRLS ad lib excitement:

MONICA

Have you got a new one?!

HETTY

Yes, the December issue. Now shush – I'm just getting to the really gory part.

HARRIET

Tell us about Mad Flora.

MONICA

Read it to us.

SARAH

Tell us, please!

HETTY

All right… But you'd better not wet yourself, Sheila.
Mad Flora Jackson was a poor servant girl and her horrid mistress scolded her all the time. So one dark night Flora took a ball of string…and the sharpest carving knife in the kitchen. She tied up her nagging mistress and then…she cut off her tongue!
And mad Flora Jackson ran away and to this day, nobody knows where she is. She might be in this very Hospital right now…

SHEILA

That wasn't very scary… Tell us another one.

HARRIET

Yes, tell us another!

MONICA

Tell us another!

HETTY

All right. I'll tell you about – The Meat Axe Murderer Man.
In a dark alley in London, there is a small butcher's shop…

Musical montage. The girls react – excited, as HETTY continues to tell her stories:

HETTY

The Baby Boiler. The Streatham Strangler…

HARRIET

Another! Another!

HETTY

> The Stoke Newington Stabber.
> Tomorrow night, I'll tell you about the murdering Matron
> and her gang of killer nurses. 'Night.

GIRLS

> 'Night...

SCENE 31 – INFLUENZA EPIDEMIC

The girls start coughing. One by one they become ill. They all sneeze.

MATRON BOTTOMLY rings the bell.

MATRON BOTTOMLY

> Time for outdoor play, girls! Off you go, run around in the
> lovely fresh air. Don't just stand there shivering!

HARRIET

> But I'm so cold, Matron.

MATRON BOTTOMLY

> Cold? Of course you're cold if you loll around like that all
> day! Take some exercise. Skip. Run. Jump. That will blow
> those horrid colds away.
> *(Rings the bell.)*
> Outside!

The GIRLS shiver outside. They try to run. It makes them sick.

All the GIRLS are sick.

HETTY staggers off, ill. The other GIRLS become NURSES.

NURSE1

> This is the worst epidemic I've ever seen.

NURSE2

> How many children are sick now?

NURSE3

> I've lost count, but we're running out of beds.

MATRON BOTTOMLY

> Fetch warm blankets. Boil more water. Burn the infected
> sheets. Ida!

IDA

> Yes, Matron?

MATRON BOTTOMLY

> Go and help in the infirmary.

HETTY FEATHER: ACT TWO

IDA
> But I'm not a nurse, Ma'am.

MATRON BOTTOMLY
> Half the hospital is down with this wretched influenza.
> We need all the help we can get.

> *IDA, MATRON BOTTOMLY and the NURSES walk around, calling out instructions.*

NURSE1
> More boiling water.

NURSE2
> We need more clean sheets.

NURSE3
> Send for the doctor.

MATRON BOTTOMLY
> Cancel all lessons. Foundlings to remain in their dormitories.

NURSE1
> More blankets.

NURSE2
> The doctor's on his way.

NURSE3
> We need help here, please!

NURSE1
> Scrub the floors with carbolic soap.

NURSE2
> One of the little boys is failing fast. He's calling for his
> mother, and brothers, and his sister.

NURSE1
> What's his sister's name?

NURSE2
> Hetty Feather.

IDA
> Hetty Feather… Hetty!

> *IDA runs over to HETTY.*

NURSE1
> We need more warm broth.

NURSE2
When will the doctor get here?

NURSE3
More hot water.

IDA
Hetty. How are you feeling now?

HETTY
Much better, thank you.

IDA
I'm so glad... Listen, Hetty. Your brother needs you.

HETTY
Gideon needs me? Why? What's happened?

IDA
You need to be a brave girl, Hetty. Your brother's very
poorly, and he's asking for you...

HETTY
But we're not allowed to see the boys.

IDA
I'm allowing it. Ssh. Don't tell no one.

HETTY
I love you, Ida.

*IDA puts a blanket around HETTY and they go to the infirmary,
where SAUL is being looked after by NURSES.*

SCENE 32 – SAUL'S DEATH

HETTY *(CONT'D.)*
Gideon? Gideon! I need to see Gideon.

NURSE1
Ssh!

NURSE2 *(Simultaneously.)*
What do you think you're doing?

HETTY
I'm looking for my brother Gideon. Gideon Smeed.

NURSE2
There's no Gideon here.

NURSE1
Quiet, girl. This is an infirmary.

HETTY *(To IDA.)*
> But you said he was asking for me.

NURSE2
> Are you Hetty Feather?

HETTY
> Yes...

NURSE1
> Your brother Saul has been asking for you.

HETTY
> Saul? Saul was asking for me?

IDA
> Poor little mite...

HETTY
> Saul? It's me, Hetty.

NURSE1
> He's very fevered. I'm not sure he'll know you.

HETTY
> Saul.

SAUL
> Go away.

HETTY
> He knows me.
> Saul. I know you don't like me. I know you wish the others
> were here instead. And most of all, I wish that Mother was
> here. And I know she'd come to see you if she could. You
> were always her favourite, you know. When she took you
> to the hospital, she was so sad. She cried for days and days,
> and nobody could comfort her...

NURSE1
> You're supposed to be cheering your brother up!

IDA
> She is...

HETTY *(To SAUL.)*
> It's true. She never smiled again. She just moped in a
> corner all day long, missing her favourite boy...

> *HETTY takes SAUL's hand. This time, he allows it.*

NURSE1
He's sleeping peacefully.

IDA
Well done, Hetty.

NURSE2 takes SAUL's crutch.

HETTY
Where are you taking that?

NURSE2
Some other little boy may need it.

HETTY
Saul needs it!

HETTY tries to grab the crutch from the NURSE.

IDA
Hetty…

HETTY
Give it back!

NURSE1
Ssh…

IDA *(To the NURSES.)*
Please…

The NURSE releases the crutch to HETTY. The NURSES move aside. HETTY places SAUL's crutch near him.

HETTY
Saul. I'm sorry.

IDA puts her arm around HETTY and takes her out.

Music. The NURSES take the pillow and blanket from SAUL's bed. He stands and looks at HETTY.

MATRON BOTTOMLY
… Let us pray for those we have lost. Our sisters, Hannah, Mary, Rebecca and Sarah; and our brothers, Charles, Mathias, and Saul.

SAUL leaves.

MATRON BOTTOMLY
Almighty God, we thank thee that it hath pleased thee to deliver them from this sinful world, into thy eternal and everlasting glory. Through Jesus Christ our Lord, Amen.

ENSEMBLE
> *I will love you all the day.*
> *In my heart you will always stay,*
> *Even if I have to stray*
> *Over the hills and far away.*
> *I will love you all the day.*
> *In my heart you will always stay,*
> *Even if I have to stray*
> *Over the hills and far away.*

IDA
You was a good sister to him, Hetty.

HETTY *(To audience.)*
I wasn't. I was a terrible sister to Saul. And now it was too late.
But I could still be a good sister to Gideon. I realised what I had
to do. Somehow, I had to get to the boys' wing and see him…

MATRON BOTTOMLY dumps a basket of clothes for HETTY.

HETTY
Every afternoon, we girls had to mend the boys' clothes.
I hated it.
(She goes through the clothes. Has an idea.)
– but then, I realised how it could be useful…
(To MATRON BOTTOMLY.)
Please Matron, may I continue with my darning? I do hate
to leave a task unfinished.

MATRON inspects HETTY's work.

MATRON BOTTOMLY
Showing diligence at last, Hetty Feather? You may make a
passable maidservant yet. You may stay and complete your
work.

HETTY
Thank you, Matron.

*MATRON leaves. HETTY grabs the boys' clothes and shoves them
under her uniform. She runs off and changes into the boys' clothes.*

SCENE 33 – HETTY GOES TO SEE GIDEON

*A bell clangs. BOYS emerge into the playground – yelling and shouting,
playing rough war games. HETTY wanders amongst them. Watching their
games. The other boys notice the 'new boy'. HETTY pretends to shoot one
of them and is accepted into their games.*

HETTY asks the boys one at a time:

HETTY
> Where's Gideon? Have you seen Gideon? Gideon Smeed?

BOY1
> You mean Idiot Boy?

HETTY
> I'm looking for Gideon Smeed.

BOY2
> That's Idiot Boy!

BOY3
> What do you want with Idiot Boy!

HETTY
> He's not an idiot. He's my brother!

BOY1
> Idiot Boy's got a brother!

BOYS *(Chant.)*
> Idiot Boy's got a brother!

HETTY
> Just tell me where he is!

BOY1
> Hiding by the bins. Like usual.

They push HETTY towards GIDEON.

HETTY finds GIDEON and runs to him. GIDEON flinches.

HETTY
> Gideon, it's me... You remember me, don't you?
> Gideon?

BOY4
> He doesn't speak.

HETTY
> Of course he speaks!

BOY2
> No he don't.

BOY3
> He's not spoke since the day he got here.

The BOYS go off to play elsewhere.

HETTY *(To GIDEON.)*
> Gideon, it's me!

He doesn't seem to recognise her:

HETTY

Remember our home? Remember Mother – and Jem –
and Saul?
*(She looks around – the boys have lost interest and moved
away.)*
Remember me – your Hetty?
(Takes her hat off.)
Your sister?

HETTY hugs GIDEON.

HETTY

Oh, Gid, it's hateful hateful hateful here isn't it?
Are they all horrid to you?
(No answer.)
You have to fight back. Promise me you will! Gideon,
please talk to me. Say something. Anything. You can call
me names. You can say, Hetty Feather is a mean, nasty,
pigface, smellybottom sister! Say it!

*The bell goes. The boys head back to class. GIDEON follows the other
boys. HETTY follows him.*

SCENE 34 – HETTY SAVES GIDEON FROM MATRON BOTTOMLY

HETTY

You don't even have to say it out loud. Just say it in your
head. But you must talk to yourself every day. Tell yourself
about home. That's what I do. I picture our house. I
picture Jem. I picture Mother… I know it hurts, but you
have to remember. If you don't, you won't be Gideon any
more. You'll just be another foundling boy…

The bell rings again.

HETTY

I have to go, Gid. But I'll be back. I promise…

HETTY turns to go but sees MATRON BOTTOMLY:

HETTY

Matron Bottomly!

MATRON BOTTOMLY

You boys. You're late for choir practice.

*HETTY and GIDEON are herded into class with the other boys, HETTY
keeping her head down.*

71

MALE TEACHER
Class, Matron Bottomly wishes to select some foundling boys to take part in the Christmas tableux vivant.

The BOYS are unenthusiastic.

MALE TEACHER
It's a great honour.

They're still unimpressed.

MATRON BOTTOMLY
Hardly angelic, are they?

She inspects the line.

MATRON BOTTOMLY
Too bold. Too small. Too plump. Too ugly…

HETTY keeps her head down – but MATRON BOTTOMLY focuses on GIDEON.

MATRON BOTTOMLY
Ah, now this boy has the appropriate air of humility. What is your name?

GIDEON looks panicked, but can't speak.

MALE TEACHER
That is Gideon Smeed.

MATRON BOTTOMLY
Why don't you answer me, Gideon Smeed?

BOY1
He don't speak.

MATRON BOTTOMLY
He will speak to me.

BOY2
He never speaks.

MALE TEACHER
I'm afraid it's true. This boy has been entirely silent since the day he arrived.

MATRON BOTTOMLY
Has he been examined by the doctor?

MALE TEACHER
Yes. He cannot find any physical cause.

MATRON BOTTOMLY
So the boy is dumb through sheer willful stubbornness.

MALE TEACHER
We cannot tell.

MATRON BOTTOMLY
I will not stand for such insolence.
(Summons GIDEON forward.)
Boy. Speak to me. Tell me your name.

GIDEON struggles to speak but can't.

MATRON BOTTOMLY
I see. Hold out your hand.

GIDEON holds out his hand, uncertainly. MATRON BOTTOMLY picks up a cane from the teacher and flexes it – about to hit him.

HETTY
No!

HETTY runs and grabs MATRON BOTTOMLY's cane. She throws it into a corner. An outraged MATRON BOTOMLY grabs her:

MATRON BOTTOMLY
Hetty Feather!

BOYS
It's a girl!

MATRON BOTTOMLY
This is no ordinary girl. This is a child of Satan. She has his Hell-red hair and his flaming temper.
(To HETTY.)
She must be taught a severe lesson.

MATRON BOTTOMLY drags HETTY out.

GIDEON
Hetty!

HETTY
Gideon! Remember! Remember what I told you!

MATRON BOTTOMLY
Silence girl! I will teach you to mend your ways.

GIDEON
Hetty!

GIDEON tries to run after HETTY, but is restrained by teachers.

SCENE 35 – THE ATTIC

MATRON BOTTOMLY flings HETTY into the attic. Planks represent the rafters.

MATRON BOTTOMLY
You will remain in this attic until that devilish fire is quenched. Pray that God makes you a better girl.

The door is slammed shut.

HETTY runs to the door.

HETTY
No! You can't leave me here. Let me out!

HETTY bangs on the door. No response. HETTY turns and sees the attic – the walls enclosing her.

HETTY sits down.

HETTY
All right. I will pray.
(She puts her hands together.)
I pray that Mad Flora Jackson comes and cuts Matron Stinking Bottomly's tongue off!

Breathing sounds. The rafters move. HETTY is scared as she remembers the story of Mad Flora:

HETTY
She will let me out, won't she? She can't just leave me here until I starve to death...and become a skeleton...
(Hears knocking sounds.)
Hello? Hello! Jem? Jem!

IDA arrives outside the attic door. She knocks:

IDA
Hetty? Are you in there?

HETTY
Ida! I'm here. Can you let me out?

IDA
I can't. That old witch has taken away the key.

HETTY
I hate her. I wish I'd hit her with that cane.

IDA

I hate her too. For two pins I'd slap her and slap her until she gave me the key, and let you out myself.

HETTY

Can you do that? Please?

IDA

I can't, Hetty. I'd lose my position.

HETTY

Then we could run away together!

IDA

But I'd never get another job without a reference. We'd end up in the workhouse.

HETTY

I'd rather be in the workhouse than here.

IDA

No you wouldn't, Hetty. It's a dreadful place.

HETTY

Have you been in the workhouse?
(No reply.)
Ida?

IDA

Yes. I was in there for three years. But I'm never going back there, and nor are you. Now, that's enough of such things. Have they given you anything to eat? Anything to sleep on?

HETTY

Nothing. Just a smelly old blanket.

IDA

Well, I tell you what. Imagine... Picture this. Take a deep breath and imagine you're safe in the kitchen with me. I've just baked some lovely fresh bread. Can you smell it?

HETTY

Yes. It smells wonderful. I didn't know you could picture, Ida!

IDA

I can do lots of things. Now shut your eyes. Picture yourself, lying on a soft feather mattress... You feel so light, it's like you're lying on a cloud. Can you feel it?

HETTY
Yes.

IDA
And under your head is a lovely, scented pillow that smells of lavender and roses, and camomile that we picked that day, and you're snuggling under a beautiful thick quilt. It's so cosy and warm and safe, isn't it? Like a great big hug...

HETTY
Don't leave me, Ida.

IDA
I won't. I'll stay here all night. I promise. So, don't worry about anything. Just fall asleep and have happy dreams... And one day, all your dreams will come true...

HETTY sleeps. Morning. MATRON BOTTOMLY enters.

MATRON BOTTOMLY
Hetty Feather. You look suitably chastened. Are you truly sorry, or must I leave you here for another day?

HETTY
No! No, I'm truly sorry, Matron.

MATRON BOTTOMLY
Yes, I believe you are. Good. Follow me. We have some new arrivals, and you older girls will have to help them to wash and dress.

SCENE 36 – ELIZA RETURNS

The GIRLS arrive, crying.

MATRON BOTTOMLY
Uniforms on, girls. Hetty Feather will help you.

HETTY helps the GIRLS to dress.

HETTY
Arms up. Turn around. Head up...

LITTLE GIRL1
Will you be my friend?

HETTY
Stop crying. Move along now.

LITTLE GIRL2
They cut my hair off.

HETTY
It'll grow back.

ELIZA gets to HETTY. She smiles as HETTY dresses her.

HETTY
Arms up. Turn around. Head up…

ELIZA
Are you Hetty Feather?

HETTY
Yes.

ELIZA
You're my sister!

ELIZA hugs HETTY. She's stunned – and realises:

HETTY
Eliza? Little Eliza?

ELIZA
Yes.

HETTY hugs ELIZA.

HETTY
I can't believe you remember me!

ELIZA
Jem told me all about you. He said you'd look after me.

HETTY
I will, I will! Oh Eliza, this place is so horrible. But now at least we've got each other.

ELIZA
Yes. But I won't be here very long.

HETTY
Why's that?

ELIZA
Because one day soon, Jem is going to come here and rescue me!

HETTY
Well, yes. Me too. But it might not be for a very long time…

JACQUELINE WILSON / EMMA REEVES

ELIZA

I know, but I don't mind waiting. Because –

HETTY

Because what?

ELIZA

It's my secret.

HETTY

Yes, but we're sisters. So we can tell each other anything.

ELIZA

Well – as soon as I'm grown up, me and Jem are going to get married. I will wear a beautiful long dress and a veil and guess where we're going to live? In our squirrel house! It's our tree house in the woods. Me and Jem used to play there all the time.

HETTY is gutted. ELIZA senses she's upset and tries to be kind.

ELIZA

But you can come and live there too if you like. I'm sure Jem won't mind.

HETTY

I don't think there'll be room for me.

ELIZA

Of course there will…

(Thinks.)

I know! You can be our servant girl!

HETTY's devastated. She knocks ELIZA off the bench.

ELIZA

Well. I've got to go to my lessons now. I'll see you later – sister.

HETTY

Jem! How could you?

JEM appears, up in the trees.

JEM

All right Hetty? What's the matter?

HETTY

You took Eliza to our place! You said you'd marry her?

JEM

> I didn't mean it. She was upset about coming here. I was just trying to cheer her up.

HETTY

> What about me? Did you mean what you said to me?

JEM

> You didn't believe all that, did you?

HETTY

> Of course I did. You promised!

JEM

> We were little children. It was just a game.

HETTY

> Not to me…

JEM

> Goodbye, Hetty.

> *JEM goes.*

HETTY

> Goodbye, Jem.

> *(To audience.)*

> All my hopes for the future – everything I'd wished for – had gone. My future was plain. I was Hetty Feather, a foundling, imprisoned in the hospital.

> I was going to be a drudge for the rest of my days…

SCENE 37 – THE KITCHEN

HETTY helps IDA in the kitchen.

IDA

> So, Cook's gone off sick, and they've put me in charge of the kitchen. And Matron Bottomly says I can choose a foundling girl to help me, and I choose you, Hetty Feather!

HETTY

> *(Flat.)*

> You want me to work in the kitchen.

IDA

We can spend all day together. I can teach you all my recipes. Don't you want to learn to cook?

HETTY

I don't care.

IDA

Well you should. Cooking's a skill to be proud of – Stir – It'll help you get a good position.

HETTY

As a servant.

IDA

Don't make that face! It's not so bad, being a servant – Salt – You can work your way up to being a cook-general – even a housekeeper –

HETTY

I don't want to be any sort of stupid servant!

IDA

Oh, really? So tell me, Miss Hetty Feather, what exactly are you going to do with your life? You'll need to earn your own living.

HETTY

I want to earn my own living! But not as a servant.

IDA

As what, then?

HETTY pictures. MADAME ADELINE appears in her imagination:

HETTY

I'm going to be…a circus rider.

IDA

A circus rider? Whatever put that idea into your head?

HETTY

My real mother.

IDA

What?

HETTY

My real mother is Madame Adeline. She's the greatest rider in the whole world.

MADAME ADELINE

Come and join me, my Little Star!

HETTY

One day she's going to come and take me away to live with her –

MADAME ADELINE

One day, my precious child.

IDA

Hetty Feather, I have never heard such nonsense in all my life.

HETTY

It's not nonsense! Madame Adeline told me so.

IDA

Did she? Or did you 'picture' it?
(HETTY doesn't reply.)
I thought so. Hetty, you're not a little child no more. You're too old for these silly daydreams. You need to be practical, work hard, make something of your life –

HETTY *(Rude.)*

Like you did?

IDA

Oh, I know you look down on me, Miss High and Mighty. But I've got a good place here. I work hard and I keep myself respectable. Now. Are you going to be a sensible girl and help me in the kitchen?

HETTY

No. I'm not being your skivvy.
(Deliberate.)
I'd rather go to the workhouse.

IDA

All right. I'll ask one of the others.

HETTY

Good!

IDA

Sheila!

IDA exits.

HETTY
Madame Adeline…

MADAME ADELINE
I'm here. I'm always here, my Little Star.

HETTY
As soon as I get a chance, I'm going to run away from this place. I'm coming to find you.

MADAME ADELINE
I will be waiting.

Music.

SCENE 38 – THE GOLDEN JUBILEE

MATRON BOTTOMLY
Girls, I have a very important announcement to make. As you all know, our beloved Queen has ruled over us for fifty glorious years. And, to celebrate her Golden Jubilee, you are all invited to a festive gathering at Hyde Park next Thursday.

The GIRLS gasp.

HETTY *(To audience.)*
Hyde Park! Outside!

MATRON BOTTOMLY
Mind your manners while you're out, Hetty Feather. All of London will be looking at us.

HETTY
Yes, Matron…

The GIRLS begin marching through London. Music.

HETTY *(To audience.)*
For the first time in years, I passed through the iron gates and out of the Foundling Hospital…
(To MATRON BOTTOMLY.)
Is that where the Queen lives?

MATRON BOTTOMLY
No, that's the British Museum. Founded in 1753 and home of the Elgin Marbles.

FOUNDLING1
Can we paddle in that fountain?

MATRON BOTTOMLY

Under no circumstances may you paddle in any
fountain.

FOUNDLING2

I need the lavatory.

MATRON BOTTOMLY

You should have gone before we left.

FOUNDLING3

I'm hungry.

MATRON BOTTOMLY

Refreshments will be provided when we reach Hyde
Park.

FOUNDLING4

Are we nearly there yet?

They arrive. Gasps of wonder from the FOUNDLINGS.

MATRON BOTTOMLY

Foundlings. You may amuse yourselves for one hour.
But you must stay within close proximity. And everyone –
(SHEILA is picking her nose. MATRON BOTTOMLY hits her.)
– everyone must report to marquee number ten at one o'
clock sharp. Do you all understand?

FOUNDLINGS

Yes, Matron.

MATRON BOTTOMLY

Well go on, then. Be off with you.

The excited FOUNDLINGS disperse.

HETTY

It was wondrous. There were merry-go-rounds, helter-
skelters, whirling chairs, swingboats – and best of all –
circuses. While the other foundlings went to the fairground,
I went straight to the circus field.

BARKER1

Roll up! Come and see Frinton's Fabulous Freaks!
We've got the boy who looks like a fish, the woman
who can sit very still and the man who can swallow his
own elbows.

HETTY

Have you got horses?

BARKER1
No.

BARKER2
Roll up, roll up. Come and see Marvo's Magnificent Miniature Menagerie. Marvel at the fleas on the flying trapeze. Chuckle at the Hamster Wheel of Death. Be amazed at our family of guinea pigs in tiny human costumes.

HETTY
Have you got an elephant?

BARKER2
No.

HETTY
I'm looking for Tanglefield's Travelling Circus.

BARKER2
That tuppenny-ha'penny gaff? They're up on Hampstead Heath.

HETTY
Hampstead Heath? Where's that?

BARKER2
About four miles north. That way. Follow the canal.

HETTY
Thank you!

HETTY runs off through the circus field – and bumps into GIDEON:

HETTY
Gideon!

GIDEON
Hetty!

HETTY hugs GIDEON.

HETTY
Why aren't you at the fairground with the others?

GIDEON
I was looking for you.

HETTY
You were looking for me?

GIDEON

You're my sister.

They hug again.

HETTY

Oh, Gid. You hate the Foundling Hospital too, don't you?

GIDEON

Yes.

HETTY

I'm sure you want to leave just as much as I do –

GIDEON *(Pulling away.)*

I don't want to leave.

HETTY

Why not?

GIDEON

They're going to make me be a soldier.

HETTY

Oh, Gideon...

GIDEON

I have dreams about it sometimes... Hetty, I don't want to go to war.

HETTY

You won't have to. You're coming with me.

GIDEON

Where are we going?

HETTY

The most wonderful place in the whole world.

GIDEON

Home? To see Mother and Jem?

HETTY

No. Somewhere even better. Tanglefield's Travelling Circus.

GIDEON

Is it within close proximity?

HETTY

No. It's four miles north. On Hampstead Heath.

GIDEON

But we have to be back by one o'clock.

HETTY

Not me. I'm never going back.

GIDEON

Hetty, you'll get in such trouble.

HETTY

Not if I don't get caught. Please Gid, come with me.

GIDEON

I can't…..

HETTY

I have to…

GIDEON

Hetty, don't go.

HETTY

Goodbye, Gideon.

HETTY parts from GIDEON.

SCENE 39 – JOURNEY TO HAMPSTEAD HEATH

HETTY runs, stopping ENSEMBLE members in her search for Hampstead Heath.

HETTY

Excuse me? Which way to Hampstead Heath?

ENSEMBLE

Hyde Park Corner, on to Marble Arch.

HETTY

Is this the way to Hampstead Heath?

ENSEMBLE

Take a left, past Baker Street.

HETTY

Hampstead Heath?

ENSEMBLE

You're on it love. Just carry on up the hill.

Eventually HETTY finds Tanglefield's Travelling circus. She hears the circus song:

ENSEMBLE

Prepare to be delighted, excited and maybe even frighted

– ooh, ah…

HETTY

Tanglefield's Travelling Circus?

CHINO

Next show's at seven. Fourpence each. No discounts no refunds.

HETTY

You're Chino the Clown!

CHINO

No I'm not. I'm on my break. Be off with you.

HETTY

Please, Mr. Chino. I need to see Madame Adeline. Is she still with the circus?

CHINO

Yes, Addie's still here. She's past it, if you ask me. But the circus is in her blood –

HETTY

It's in my blood, too. She's my mother.

CHINO

Your mother? You're Addie's girl?

HETTY

Yes. Where is she?

CHINO

Green wagon. Over there.

SCENE 40 – HETTY MEETS MADAME ADELINE AGAIN

HETTY goes over to the wagon and knocks. MADAME ADELINE opens the door. She seems older, and has a rough British accent.

HETTY

Hello? 'Scuse me? Hello? Madame Adeline?

MADAME ADELINE

What?

HETTY

I'm looking for Madame Adeline!

MADAME ADELINE

Yes, what d'you want?

HETTY

I'm sorry to disturb you. I'm looking for Madame Adeline.

MADAME ADELINE
What do you want with her?

HETTY
She's my mother.

MADAME ADELINE
Your mother? – Who are you?

HETTY
Hetty Feather. But that's not my real name.

MADAME ADELINE
Well, Hetty Feather. I think you'd better sit down.

HETTY sits down.

HETTY
Where is Madame Adeline? Is she here?

MADAME ADELINE
Yes, she's here.

HETTY
Can I see her?

MADAME ADELINE
You want to see Madame Adeline?

HETTY
Yes please. I need to see her right now. It's extremely
urgent.

MADAME ADELINE
Maybe this will help…

MADAME ADELINE puts on her red wig. She strikes a dramatic pose.

MADAME ADELINE *(Russian accent.)*
Ha! It is I, the great Madame Adeline herself!

HETTY
You're Madame Adeline?

MADAME ADELINE
What, don't you recognise your own mother?

HETTY stares at the real MADAME ADELINE, her dreams in tatters. She backs away:

HETTY

I'm sorry… I've made a terrible mistake…

MADAME ADELINE

Oy! Come back! Come here. I'm sorry. I didn't mean to upset you… Sit down. Come on, I don't bite. Now, tell me. What makes you think that I am your mother?

HETTY

You did… You came to our village, and I rode with you. You called me your Little Star, and precious child, and you had red hair, just like mine, and… You were so kind to me, and I thought – I wanted – I just hoped so much…

MADAME ADELINE

Don't you have a mother of your own, Hetty?

HETTY

No. I'm a foundling. I live in a horrible hospital and I never knew who my mother was…

MADAME ADELINE

Ssh ssh ssh, it's all right…
(As HETTY gradually recovers.)
Ssh… There, now. Let's get you a nice cup of tea and some cake. Everything's better with cake.

MADAME ADELINE tries to get the tea but HETTY stops her:

HETTY

I wish you were my real mother.

MADAME ADELINE

In another life, maybe…

HETTY

We could just pretend I'm your daughter! I could stay with you and feed your horses and mend your costumes…

MADAME ADELINE

No, no, no. The circus is no life for a child. Terrible things happen to girls like you.

HETTY

But I've got nowhere else to go.

MADAME ADELINE

They'd never let me keep you. They'd say I'd abducted you and set the rozzers on me. Nobody trusts circus folk. And rightly so.

HETTY

No one listens to founding children…

MADAME ADELINE

Why don't you come and see the show first? Then I'll take you back myself.

HETTY

Thank you.

MADAME ADELINE

Good girl.

MADAME ADELINE goes to prepare for the next show…

HETTY

I went to the circus and I saw Madame Adeline ride for the last time. But before the show was over, I slipped away. Nothing in the world could make me go back to the Foundling Hospital. I had to fend for myself.
(Runs through streets.)
Alone, in the great city of London…

HETTY runs through London. She dodges through the streets. Hides in a doorway.

SCENE 41 – LOST IN LONDON

HETTY finds herself in a bustling market. STREET TRADERS are selling their wares.

SISSY

Clear off you! This is my patch! Go on, find your own place.
(To punters.)
Posy for your lady, Sir.

HETTY goes away – and bumps into a GENTLEMAN, knocking his hat off:

HETTY

Oh, I'm sorry – sorry, sir –

GENTLEMAN

No harm done, my dear. Are you all right?

HETTY

I'm fine. Thank you, Sir.

GENTLEMAN

Are you lost? Where are your mother and father?

HETTY

I'm just on my way home to them.

GENTLEMAN

I see… But you look famished, my dear. Before you go, let me buy you a hot meal.

HETTY is tempted.

GENTLEMAN

Or – even better, why not come home with me? My house is just around the corner. I have a lovely warm, roaring fire, and Cook's been baking pies.

HETTY

No, I don't think so, thank you.

GENTLEMAN

I insist! Come home with me…

HETTY

No!

GENTLEMAN

I'll look after you.

HETTY

Don't touch me. Leave me alone –

He tries to pick her up.

HETTY

No! Get off me!

GENTLEMAN

Hush, Little Miss. You'll be safe with me.

HETTY

LET ME GO!

SISSY

Let her go!

SISSY grabs HETTY and throws a stone at the GENTLEMAN.

SISSY *(To HETTY.)*

Run!

SISSY and HETTY run off together.

HETTY

Thank you! Thank you…

SISSY

You stupid girl! What was you doing?

HETTY

I couldn't get away.

SISSY

You yell out and give 'em a good kicking, that's what you do. If you don't know that, you've got no business being on the streets at all.

HETTY

But I've got nowhere else to go…

SISSY looks her up and down.

SISSY

You're from that Foundling Hospital, ain't you? A woman's been round here looking for you.

HETTY

That'll be Matron Bottomly. Don't tell her where I am. I've run away.

SISSY

Have you now? Listen – you don't want to stay round here. It's not safe for a young 'un like you.

HETTY

You're not much older than me.

SISSY

I'm fourteen! Trust me, you don't want this life. If I was you, I'd get back to that Foundling Hospital. At least it's a roof over your head –

HETTY

I'm never going back there.
(Determined.)
I'd rather beg on the streets.

SISSY

All right.

SISSY hands HETTY her basket of flowers.

SISSY
Here. Take these. Get what you can for them.

HETTY
But can't you help me – ?

SISSY
Good luck, young 'un.

SISSY runs off. HETTY looks at the flowers – working out what to do next.

As people pass by, HETTY approaches them:

HETTY
Please sir, a penny for a posy?

She's ignored. She approaches the next person:

HETTY
Miss, Miss, could I trouble you –

She's snubbed again.

HETTY
Please – just a penny? –

HETTY thinks. She changes her tactics:

HETTY
Please! You must buy my flowers! I need gin money for my cruel mistress, Matron Bottomly. If she doesn't get it, she will beat me senseless!

PASSERS-BY
Awwww…

The PASSERS-BY throw money to HETTY. She counts it – pleased with her success.

HETTY
Oh, thank you, Sir. Thank you, Ma'am… And then there's me sister Sheila, she's got the smallpox and is hideously disfigured. And she's also terribly dim-witted…

The PASSERS-BY throw more money.

HETTY *(Pleased.)*
Oh, thank you… Thank you, Sir…

URCHIN1
Oy, Miss! You're getting the hang of this ain't ya? Doing well?

HETTY
Yes...

While HETTY's distracted, URCHIN2 runs past and steals HETTY's money. URCHIN1 takes the flowers. HETTY gives chase.

HETTY
Give me back my money!

HETTY is hit and falls to the floor. IDA enters, searching.

IDA
Hetty? Hetty? Excuse me, have you seen a red-headed girl..? Hetty? Hetty Feather?
(IDA finds HETTY.)
Oh, Hetty!

HETTY
Ida? Ida! How did you find me?

IDA
The flower girl told me you was here. I've been searching the streets all day and all night – I was imagining all sorts of terrible things – I've been fair demented – Never, never, never do this again, do you hear me?

HETTY
I didn't think you cared so much about me.

IDA *(In tears.)*
Oh, Hetty...

HETTY
Ida, don't! Please, don't...

HETTY hugs IDA.

IDA
My own Hetty – my own child...

HETTY
What did you say?

IDA
Nothing – nothing.

HETTY
You called me your own child...

IDA produces the receipt from the Foundling Hospital.

IDA
... Did you never guess?

HETTY

No…

IDA

I'm so sorry…

HETTY

Why would you be sorry?

IDA

I'm not the mother you hoped for. I'm just…me.

HETTY

You're the best, most wonderful mother I could ever imagine.

IDA

Really?

HETTY

Yes. But…

IDA

… What?

HETTY

… Why don't you have red hair?

IDA

It comes from your father's side…

SCENE 42 – IDA AND BOBBY

BOBBY and HETTY's MOTHER perform an aerial routine as IDA tells her story:

HETTY

Tell me about my father…

IDA

Your father was the brightest, most handsomest boy in the village. All the girls chased him. But I never did. He chased me.

He told me he'd never met anyone like me. So sweet, and so spirited. That's what he said. Oh, I led him a merry dance. I don't know if he ever knew how much I cared for him. But I loved him with all my heart…

BOBBY and IDA climb and spin. BOBBY leaves.

IDA

And then he left to go away to sea. I promised I'd wait for
him and I did. I waited and waited – and then I realised I
was going to have his baby.

HETTY

Me…

IDA

Yes, you. You were so precious – but so tiny. I couldn't
look after you. I nearly lost my mind when I had to
give you up – I ended up in the workhouse – but then, I
managed to get a job at the Foundling Hospital.

HETTY

To be with me.

IDA

Yes. All I ever wanted was to give you a true mother's love.
It's been such a torment – but such a joy, too, Hetty…

HETTY

Say my name. My real name. The one you gave me when
I was a baby.

IDA

Your eyes were so blue…so I gave you a fanciful pet name.
I called you my little Sapphire.

SCENE 43 – FINALE

HETTY

Sapphire…

HETTY returns to her hoop.

HETTY *(To audience.)*

My name is Sapphire Battersea, and this is where my story
ends – for now. Mother and I went back to the Foundling
Hospital. I was afraid I was going to get punished, but
Mother had a clever plan.

IDA

Oh no, you're mistaken, Ma'am. Hetty never ran away.
She was kidnapped by a gang of ruffians in Hyde Park.
Gideon Smeed saw the whole thing.

GIDEON

I saw the whole thing.

HETTY

So here we are, back at the Foundling Hospital. And Madame Adeline herself came to visit me!

MADAME ADELINE

One day we'll meet again – my little star.

HETTY

Matron Bottomly still hates the very sight of me.

MATRON BOTTOMLY

As scarlet and sinful as your hair. You'll come to a bad end, mark my words.

HETTY

I know you'd like that. But I don't think I will. I'm going to publish my life story and I'll earn lots of money and buy a fine house and live there with Mother.

GIDEON

Can I live with you too? I don't want to go into the army.

HETTY

Of course you can Giddy, you can be anything you want to be.

GIDEON

I'd like to be a servant girl.

HETTY

I'd like to picture happy endings for everyone. I could picture me and Jem, back together again…

JEM

Hetty, I meant everything I said. One day I'm going to come and find you. I promise.

HETTY

Yes, I could picture that. And I could picture Saul alive again.

SAUL

Thanks Hetty. I thought you'd forgotten me.

HETTY

I'll never forget you Saul. You'll always be alive in my memory.

SAUL

I suppose that'll have to do.

HETTY *(To audience.)*

But this isn't a fairy story. It's my own, real life. And in real life, people don't always live happily ever after.
(To IDA.)
But we will.

IDA

Will we, Hetty? – Sapphire??

HETTY

Yes, Mother. I am absolutely certain.

HETTY hangs upside down from her hoop, triumphant. Multi-coloured feathers fall on her.

The MUSICIANS join the actors to take their bows.

ENSEMBLE *(Song.)*
Were I laid on Greenland's shore
Or in the burning Indian sun
Should I never see you more
Still we two will be as one

And I will love you all the day
In my heart you will always stay
Even if I have to stray
Over the hills and far away

Since the day that I was born
You have always been with me
Every place I've ever gone,
Everywhere that I will be.

And I will love you all the day
In my heart you will always stay
Even if I have to stray
Over the hills and far away

by the same author

Cool Hand Luke
Donn Pearce
9781849431651

Carrie's War
Nina Bawden
9781840027204

Anne of Green Gables
L.M Montgomery
9781840025385

Little Women
Louisa May Alcott
9781840025231

WWW.OBERONBOOKS.COM

Follow us on www.twitter.com/@oberonbooks
& www.facebook.com/OberonBooksLondon

Lightning Source UK Ltd.
Milton Keynes UK
UKHW020045101120
373096UK00006B/399